THE LIVING GOSPEL

Daily Devotions for Advent 2017

Charles Paolino

AVE MARIA PRESS AVE Notre Dame, Indiana

Founded in 1865, Ave Maria Press is a ministry of the United States Province of Holy Cross.

www.avemariapress.com

Paperback: ISBN-13 978-1-59471-765-9

E-book: ISBN-13 978-1-59471-766-6

Cover image "Approaching Bethlehem" © 2012 by Jeni Butler, artworkbyjeni.wix.com/art.

Cover and text design by John R. Carson.

Printed and bound in the United States of America.

Introduction

One of my Advent rituals is rereading Charles Dickens's 1843 novella *A Christmas Carol*. Commentaries on this story often remark that Dickens influenced the way Christmas has been observed ever since he wrote this classic: festive family gatherings, sumptuous meals, gift giving, caroling, and churchgoing. I have also read that there is a long-standing debate as to whether the story bears a Christian message, but to me it clearly does.

In one disturbing passage, for example, the ghost of Jacob Marley shows his former business partner, Ebenezer Scrooge, the spirits of the dead who, like Marley himself, hadn't lifted a finger in life to assist the poor:

> The air was filled with phantoms, wandering hither and thither in restless haste, and moaning as they went. . . . Many had been personally known to Scrooge in their lives. He had been quite familiar with one old ghost . . . who cried piteously at being unable to assist a wretched woman with an infant, whom it saw below, upon a door-step. The misery with them all was, clearly, that they sought to interfere, for good, in human matters, and had lost the power for ever.

Marley describes his own torment:

> It is required of every man that the spirit within him should walk abroad among his fellow-men, and travel far and wide; and if that spirit goes not forth in life, it is condemned to do so after death. It is doomed to wander through the world—oh, woe is me!—and witness what it cannot share, but might have shared

on earth, and turned to happiness! . . . Why did I
walk through crowds of fellow-beings with my eyes
turned down, and never raise them to that blessed
Star which led the Wise Men to a poor abode? Were
there no poor homes to which its light would have
conducted me!

A Christian message? I think so. How often have we
heard from Pope Francis about our mission to get out
of our comfort zones and go to the edges of society to
bring comfort and sustenance and justice?

But *A Christmas Carol* is not pessimistic; its central
figure is not one of the dead who wasted life's opportunities but rather one of the living, Scrooge, who responded
to what I say was a Christian message by reviewing and
reforming his life.

This small book of reflections is an invitation for
you to pause each day of Advent—perhaps for ten
minutes—to meditate on the meaning of this season and the coming feast and the application of both
to your daily life. For each day of Advent there are
prompts for prayer, including a passage from the
Responsorial Psalm or other scripture read at that
day's Mass; a verse or two from the gospel reading
for that day; a personal reflection inspired by that passage; a suggested step toward spiritual growth; and
a closing prayer.

Using this little book at the same time of day and
in the same quiet place—perhaps before your Advent
wreath—can help you to build some calm and rhythm
into the season.

Marley's ghost and the spirits of Christmas provided
Scrooge with his first Advent; they got him to pause and
think about his life, and he came to see that the spirit of
Christmas was not about celebrating a holiday but about

giving away one's life every day of the year. As Dickens wrote in the conclusion of his story, "May that be truly said of us, and all of us."

SUNDAY, DECEMBER 3
FIRST WEEK OF ADVENT

BEGIN

Be silent. Be still. Pray, "Come, Lord Jesus!"

PRAY

While you wrought awesome deeds we could not
hope for, such as they had not heard of from of old.
No ear has ever heard, no eye ever seen,
any God but you
doing such deeds for those who wait for him.

~Isaiah 64:2–4

LISTEN

Read Mark 13:33–37.

Jesus said to his disciples: "Be watchful! Be alert!"

~Mark 13:33

Let Us Awaken

Baseball has added many expressions to our everyday language, including the term "benchwarmer," which was used in baseball journalism at least as early as 1890.

That term refers to a team member who does not play regularly. "Benchwarmer" can suggest a player who is inferior to the regulars and, consequently, of little value to the team, but in many cases, the opposite is true. The benchwarmer may be a player of great value in strategic situations. For example, a batter who has a knack for bunting in order to drive in a runner home from third base.

The most sought-after benchwarmer—known more formally as a "reserve player"—is one who is always in the game, even when he's sitting on the bench. He is always alert and attentive to the situation on the field so that, if he is called into the game, he is ready. He is not the player lounging against the wall; he is the player on the edge of his seat. That's what Jesus is urging for his disciples in today's gospel passage.

Some commentators use this passage to warn us to be ready for the final judgment at the end of time, but we needn't focus on only that as Advent begins. We can also take Jesus' remarks as an invitation to awaken our spiritual consciousness, to become aware, all day every day, of God's love for us—a love so great that he was willing to join his divine nature and our human nature in the birth of our Savior.

Christmas is only three weeks away. Wake up now to the wonder of the incarnation, and never be distracted from it as the holy day draws near.

ACT

I will try to avoid unnecessary busyness during this season and, instead, open myself each day to quiet anticipation of the Lord's coming.

PRAY

Lord Jesus Christ, may I never lose a sense of wonder and gratitude for the great gift of your incarnation. May my anticipation of your coming absorb me throughout this holy season. Amen.

Monday, December 4
First Week of Advent

BEGIN

Be silent. Be still. Pray, "Come, Lord Jesus!"

PRAY

They shall beat their swords into plowshares
and their spears into pruning hooks;
One nation shall not raise the sword against another,
nor shall they train for war again.

~Isaiah 2:4

LISTEN

Read Matthew 8:5–11.

The centurion said in reply, "Lord, I am not worthy to
have you enter under my roof; only say the word and
my servant will be healed."

~Matthew 8:8

Brothers, Sisters All

The television series *Downton Abbey* presented a picture
of life in a British manor house in the early twentieth
century. The titled residents treated their servants with
respect and kindness and often even intervened to make
a servant's life better. But historians tell us that the situation was usually quite different from this.

Servants commonly lived and worked in harsh conditions and were kept away from the family as much as
possible. There were usually separate staircases to min-
imize encounters between the householders and those
"below stairs," and a servant who did happen to cross

paths with one of the lords or ladies was to turn and face the wall until the grand personage had passed by.

This sort of thing was to be expected in a society with sharp class distinctions, and the absence of such a mentality is an interesting aspect to today's gospel passage. Jesus remarks that he has never found in Israel the level of faith exhibited by the centurion who begged Jesus to heal an ailing servant.

No doubt, Jesus is referring in part to the fact that the centurion, a Gentile and an agent of the Roman occupation, would approach him at all, and the fact that the centurion believed that Jesus could heal the servant just by willing it.

But Jesus must have been moved too by the soldier's concern for a "serving boy" who would have been beneath the notice of most Roman officers but whose life was as dear as any other in the eyes of God. The implication is that the centurion had already embraced the kind of compassion Jesus preached and practiced—a compassion without distinction that all Christian disciples are called to imitate.

ACT

I will resist any inclination to regard the life or well-being of another as less precious than my own.

PRAY

Almighty God, may I be inspired by the centurion's encounter with Jesus to attend to the well-being of those I encounter this day. May I respect each person and respond to him or her in love. Amen.

Tuesday, December 5
First Week of Advent

BEGIN

Be silent. Be still. Pray, "Come, Lord Jesus!"

PRAY

The calf and the young lion shall browse together,
with a little child to guide them.

~Isaiah 11:6

LISTEN

Read Luke 10:21–24.

I give you praise, Father, Lord of heaven and earth,
for although you have hidden these things from the
wise and the learned you have revealed them to the
childlike.

~Luke 10:21

Mouths of Babes

I was vesting for a First Communion Mass when one
of the altar servers, a boy, told me that I had given him
a box of crayons at his First Communion Mass a year
before. I had used the box of crayons, which had lain
unopened in my dresser drawer for fifteen years, as a
prop in my homily to the children.

"You said," the boy reminded me, "that if you have
something with some value but never use it for what it
was made for, it is worthless."

"I was at that Mass," said another server, a girl. "You
said it was like your heart: if you keep it inside you, it
has no value. You have to give it away."

"Yeah," said the boy, "and that's what Jesus did."

I was dazzled by these two kids, and only later did it occur to me what an apt metaphor that conversation was for the point Jesus made at the beginning of today's gospel passage. The idea that those children had absorbed is both profound and simple, and its beauty is in its simplicity.

Scholars in theology, philosophy, and scripture make essential contributions, but applying our faith to everyday life and imparting it to others in our role as missionary disciples requires a grasp of the core of Jesus' message—the greatest commandments: Love God and love each other—without conditions or exceptions.

The learned and the clever often see conditions and exceptions; the merest children, regardless of their age, do not.

ACT

Jesus said the whole law is summed up in the "greatest commandments" (Matthew 22:36–40). Each evening this week, I will reflect on how well I lived those commandments throughout my day.

PRAY

Come Holy Spirit, clear my mind of distractions, and prepare me to see clearly how the commandments of love can transform my life and the lives of everyone I encounter. Amen.

WEDNESDAY, DECEMBER 6
FIRST WEEK OF ADVENT

BEGIN

Be silent. Be still. Pray, "Come, Lord Jesus!"

PRAY

> You spread the table before me
> in the sight of my foes;
> You anoint my head with oil;
> my cup overflows.

~Psalm 23:5

LISTEN

Read Matthew 15:29–37.

> He took the seven loaves and the fish, gave thanks,
> broke the loaves, and gave them to the disciples, who
> in turn gave them to the crowds. They all ate and
> were satisfied.

~Matthew 15:36–37

How Many Loaves?

My family and I were driving across a desert in the West many years ago, staring out at the stark, brown landscape, broken only by sagebrush, tumbleweed, and the occasional prairie dog. After regarding this scene in silence for a while, my father-in-law remarked, "If this were Israel, there would be corn growing here." I knew what he meant; I had seen firsthand the outcomes of agricultural programs in Israel. I also think of his comment whenever I read the story in today's gospel passage about Jesus feeding the multitude.

In this episode and in others like it that are described in the gospels, Jesus wasn't showing off his power over nature; he was teaching us that we can provide food for the hungry if we really want to—a constant theme in the ministry of Pope Francis. Hunger-related problems are not caused by lack of ample food supply but by our failing to justly distribute what we produce, limit waste, curtail excess consumption, protect the environment, reexamine priorities in production and distribution, and understand adequate nourishment as a human right, not as a privilege of the few.

Those are big challenges that require big changes in business practices and public policy, but as citizens we are not altogether powerless to influence decision makers. We must as a global community be willing to make changes. There are plenty of hungry people in our spheres of influence, and there are plenty of ways for us to do as Jesus did by making the most of what we have at hand—using only what we need and sharing all we can.

ACT

I will research the degree to which hunger is a problem in my community, county, or state and then commit myself to do one concrete thing to help curtail or eliminate it.

PRAY

Creator God, you did not entrust the earth's resources to human beings so that each of us could take advantage of them only for our own benefit. As a disciple of Jesus—who fed the hungry when others failed—may I share all I can with those who are in need. Amen.

Thursday, December 7
First Week of Advent (Memorial of St. Ambrose)

BEGIN

Be silent. Be still. Pray, "Come, Lord Jesus!"

PRAY

Give thanks to the Lord, for he is good,
for his mercy endures forever.

~Psalm 118:1

LISTEN

Read Matthew 7:21, 24–27.

"Everyone who listens to these words of mine and
acts on them will be like a wise man who built his
house on rock."

~Matthew 7:24

Go Tell It

In the liturgy today, the Church remembers St. Ambrose,
a fourth-century Roman Christian who served as bishop
of Milan.

Ambrose was revered for his charity and his schol-
arship, and he was an influential preacher. His preaching and counsel had a particularly powerful impact on
Augustine of Hippo; in fact, Ambrose played a major
role in dispelling Augustine's skepticism about Chris-
tianity. In AD 347, Ambrose baptized Augustine, the
future bishop, spiritual writer, and saint.

The names Ambrose and Augustine are among the
most prominent in the history of the Church; these men
were giants. While we who are Christian today may not

be called to be bishops, theologians, and preachers, we are called to imitate Ambrose—according to our abilities—by witnessing to our faith so as to make it attractive to those who have left it or have never embraced it. This season provides an especially good opportunity for us to take on this evangelizing role.

The manner in which we observe Advent and prepare for Christmas can be a sign to others that Jesus Christ, and no other aspect of the preparation and celebration, is at the center of our lives and is the inspiration for everything else we do.

The reverence and joy with which we practice our faith—and our gentle invitations to join us—may do more than all the lawn signs and bumper stickers in the world to touch other people's hearts and draw them closer to the Lord, maybe even to help them return to church or come for the first time.

ACT

I will be alert for opportunities to share with others the spiritual meaning this season has for me—joyful expectation of the coming of the Savior.

PRAY

Lord Jesus, you sent your first disciples to spread the Good News to friends and strangers. Through prayer and charity, may I continue their mission during this holy season, touching the hearts of friends and strangers and drawing them closer to you. Amen.

Friday, December 8

Solemnity of the Immaculate Conception

BEGIN

Be silent. Be still. Pray, "Come, Lord Jesus!"

PRAY

In him we were also chosen, destined in accord with
the purpose of the One who accomplishes all things
according to the attention of his will, so that we
might exist for the praise of his glory, we who first
hoped in Christ.

~Ephesians 1:11–12

LISTEN

Read Luke 1:26–38.

Mary said, "Behold, I am the handmaid of the Lord.
May it be done to me according to your word."

~Luke 1:38

"Thy Will Be Done"

Thomas Aquinas wrote that within humankind "is
both the powerful surge toward the good because we
are made in the image of God, and the darker impulses
toward evil because of the effects of original sin." We
are cleansed of original sin in baptism, but we remain
free to exercise our will either in tune with or contrary
to the will of God.

There have been two exceptions to the stain of original sin. Jesus, conceived by the Holy Spirit, was not
touched by original sin; and Mary, his mother, was conceived without the mark of original sin—that's what
we celebrate today: the immaculate conception of Mary.

The Church believes that Mary was given this privilege because she was to be the vessel through which God would enter human history.

But Mary still had a free will. And we see her exercising that free will in the event described in the passage from St. Luke's gospel. The angel presents her with astounding news—although she is a virgin, she will bear a son—and Mary freely answers, "May it be done to me according to your word." In other words, not my will but your will be done.

The Church teaches us that throughout her life, Mary always exercised her free will in keeping with what she understood to be the will of God. She is dear to us, because she is the mother of Jesus, our Savior. But she is also the model, the ideal, of the kind of life every one of us can strive for. As first disciple, Mary's example and ongoing help is our sure and steady guide for the Christian life.

Even if we falter, as we will, we can begin again by recalling this unique and holy woman and join her in praying to our Father: your will be done on earth as it is in heaven.

ACT

Today I will listen for God's will for me. I will carve out quiet space to pray and attend to what elements of the Christian life I find it hard to say yes to. I will pray that I may have the grace needed to respond as Mary did, choosing to trust and to rejoice that God calls me to do good.

PRAY

Creator God, you have made me in your likeness by the gifts of understanding and free will. May I, like the Blessed Mother, respond to your love and generosity by always saying yes to your divine will. Amen.

Saturday, December 9

First Week of Advent

BEGIN

Be silent. Be still. Pray, "Come, Lord Jesus!"

PRAY

With your own eyes you shall see your Teacher,
While from behind, a voice shall sound in your ears:
"This is the way; walk in it."

~Isaiah 30:20–21

LISTEN

Read Matthew 9:35–10:1, 5a, 6–8.

"Without cost you have received; without cost you
are to give."

~Matthew 10:8

The Gift Is You

As Christmas approached in 2013, it appeared that it would be the last for eight-year-old Delaney Brown of West Reading, Pennsylvania. She had been diagnosed earlier that year with a rare form of leukemia that did not respond to treatment. One of Delaney's "bucket list" wishes was to hear Christmas carolers outside her home.

On the night of December 22, in Delaney's home town of about 4,200 residents, thousands of people fulfilled that wish. A crowd of between five and ten thousand friends, family, and strangers gathered to sing for her. As they sang, an image of Delaney appeared on the "Team Laney" Facebook page: she was giving thumbs up with the message, "I can hear you now! Love you!" Delaney died on Christmas morning.

The many people who learned about Delaney through campaigns to assist her family could give nothing that would save her life. But they did have songs, and on that winter night, those songs were worth more than tons of gold. A song told Delaney that thousands of people, most of whom had never met her, loved her enough to give the only thing they had to offer.

Like the first disciples of Jesus, every one of us has gifts that can ease the pain, lighten the burden, or cheer the heart of someone. It may be a large check; it may be a hot meal or a gift card; it may be a voice on the phone or a signature on a note; or it may be a song.

And Jesus says to us as he did to his first followers, "Without cost you have received; without cost you are to give."

ACT

Today I will do at least one act of kindness to bring a little joy, comfort, or encouragement to another. I will continue to hold that person in prayer throughout the day.

PRAY

Lord Jesus, I am but one of your followers and my abilities are limited. But may I be a blessing to the world this day by freely sharing the gifts and talents you have given to me to share. Amen.

Sunday, December 10
Second Week of Advent

BEGIN

Be silent. Be still. Pray, "Come, Lord Jesus!"

PRAY

The Lord does not delay his promise, as some regard
"delay," but he is patient with you,
not wishing that any should perish
but that all should come to repentance.

~2 Peter 3:9

LISTEN

Read Mark 1:1–8.

"I am sending my messenger ahead of you;
he will prepare your way.
A voice of one crying out in the desert:
'Prepare the way of the Lord,
make straight his paths.'"

~Mark 1:2–3

Wake-Up Call

An acquaintance once shared with me a handwritten
register from the Packer House, an old hotel in Perth
Amboy, New Jersey, that burned down in 1969. Perth
Amboy was on the vaudeville circuits in the 1920s and
'30s, and the names of some of the stage performers
were listed in the Packer House register. Also listed
were "advance men" who, as the name implied, visited
a theater town ahead of the acts and made whatever
arrangements were necessary, including wake-up calls.

In a way John the Baptist was the original advance man—preparing the people of the Judean countryside and Jerusalem for the ministry of Jesus. He was a living, breathing wake-up call. John is described in the gospels as a rugged firebrand, and his appearance, manner, and language no doubt shook up many listeners, but at the heart of his message was repentance and forgiveness of sins.

Advent is the season of John, the baptizer and advance man, when he urges us, as he did the people of his own time, to prepare to receive Jesus today—and to meet Jesus at the end of time—by taking stock of ourselves, changing what needs to be changed, and beginning a new relationship with God.

Advent is not a penitential season as is Lent, and yet it invites spiritual renewal, an opportunity, as John said, to "reform" our lives, not necessarily by undergoing dramatic conversion, but by sincerely pondering changes in priorities and habits, and acting on them, thereby growing closer to Christ.

ACT

Today I will find out when confessions are available at my parish church and schedule a time to receive the Sacrament of Reconciliation to help prepare my heart for the coming of Jesus.

PRAY

Almighty God, John the Baptist announced the coming of your Son, Jesus Christ, with a tone of urgency and a call for penitence that leads to forgiveness. May I always be willing to probe my conscience and reform my life in order to draw closer to you. Amen.

Monday, December 11
Second Week of Advent

BEGIN

Be silent. Be still. Pray, "Come, Lord Jesus!"

PRAY

Strengthen the hands that are feeble,
make firm the knees that are weak,
say to those whose hearts are frightened:
Be strong, fear not!

~Isaiah 35:3–4

LISTEN

Read Luke 5:17–26.

When Jesus saw their faith, he said, "As for you, your
sins are forgiven."

~Luke 5:20

First Things First

In his television movie *Jesus of Nazareth*, Franco Zeffirelli
places the miracle described in today's gospel passage in
the house of Simon the fisherman before Simon became
Peter the apostle. Simon is annoyed when friends of the
paralyzed man remove a part of the roof to lower the
stretcher close to Jesus. The implication is that Simon is
more concerned with his roof than with the well-being
of the disabled man. Eventually, of course, Simon Peter
gets his priorities straight.

Jesus' own priorities in this episode are also worth
noting. When he witnesses the faith of the men who went
to so much trouble to get their friend into the house, his
first concern is not for what might seem obvious—the

fellow's disability—but rather for the man's spiritual life: "As for you, your sins are forgiven."

The gospel tells us that the critics of Jesus raised the usual issue, that only God can forgive sins, but we can imagine that the others present—and especially the men who brought the paralytic—may have been flummoxed when Jesus didn't deal with the man's pitiable condition.

Ultimately, Jesus in his compassion does heal the man, but first he teaches the critical lesson that all of us need more than anything else, forgiveness for our sins so we can live at peace with God now and forever.

ACT

I will spend a few minutes today calling to mind someone who has hurt me and whom I have not fully forgiven. I will pray for the will to forgive him or her and chart a path toward reconciliation.

PRAY

Almighty God, I believe that when I come to you in penance, you will forgive my sins. Thank you for this grace that I receive because of the ministry, passion, and resurrection of your son, Jesus Christ. Amen.

TUESDAY, DECEMBER 12
FEAST OF OUR LADY OF GUADALUPE

BEGIN

Be silent. Be still. Pray, "Come, Lord Jesus!"

PRAY

God's temple in heaven was opened,
and the ark of his covenant could be seen in the
temple.

A great sign appeared in the sky, a woman clothed
with the sun,
with the moon under her feet,
and on her head a crown of twelve stars.

~Revelation 11:19a–12:1

LISTEN

Read Luke 1:39–45.

"Most blessed are you among women,
and blessed is the fruit of your womb. . . .
Blessed are you who believed
that what was spoken to you by the Lord
would be fulfilled."

~Luke 1:42,45

Mary, Our Mother

The feast that the Church celebrates today evolved from
several apparitions of the Virgin Mary reported in the
sixteenth century by Juan Diego, a Mexican peasant who
became the first indigenous person from the Americas to
be canonized. By Juan Diego's account, the Virgin had
appeared to him three times and had promised to meet
him again. Before the time appointed for that fourth

visitation, however, Juan Diego become preoccupied with attending to his uncle, Juan Bernardino, who had fallen ill.

As Juan Diego was en route to fetch a priest to administer sacraments to the ailing man, the Virgin intercepted him, and when Juan Diego explained himself, she asked, "*¿No estoy yo aquí que soy tu madre?*" (Am I not here, I who am your mother?) Juan Bernardino was restored to health and reported that he too had seen the Virgin, at his bedside.

"Am I not here . . . your mother?" That's a good question to remember during this Advent season—the season of Mary's expectation—and a good question to ponder at any time.

The Church is devoted to Mary as the Mother of God; as the first disciple of her son, Jesus; and as our intercessor par excellence. Why overlook her when we are seeking help or comfort for others or ourselves? Who better to intercede with God on our behalf than the woman who accepted unconditionally God's plan that she should give birth to the Christ?

ACT

I will choose one Marian devotion today and plan a way to make it a regular part of my prayer life. If I already practice a Marian devotion, I will try to discover some aspect of it that I do not now know.

PRAY

O Blessed Virgin Mary, I turn to you as a mother and ask you to bring to your glorified Son my petitions for peace and justice among the nations of the world. Amen.

Wednesday, December 13
Second Week of Advent

BEGIN

Be silent. Be still. Pray, "Come, Lord Jesus!"

PRAY

He pardons all your iniquities,
he heals all your ills.
He redeems your life from destruction,
he crowns you with kindness and compassion.

~Psalm 103:3–4

LISTEN

Read Matthew 11:28–30.

"Take my yoke upon you and learn from me,
for I am meek and humble of heart."

~Matthew 11:29

The Right of Way

I was driving to work one day and being irritated by a driver behind me who was staying far too close to my car. I could tell by the way the woman appeared in my rearview mirror and by the way she kept crowding me that she was impatient, and I couldn't understand why she didn't pass me on the left. After about a half mile of this, the driver abruptly pulled over to the *right* and passed me on the shoulder. Then, about a half dozen car lengths in front of me, she pulled into a donut shop.

God bless her. I hope she enjoyed the donut, took the coffee without caffeine, and safely got to her ultimate destination. If this incident were isolated, it would be trivial. Unfortunately, it was not isolated but one of many dangerous maneuvers one is likely to see on the roads on any day in my part of the country.

Commentaries on today's gospel reading usually fix on the heavy burden and the metaphor of the yoke, but many of us would profit from taking to heart this clause: "learn from me, for I am meek and humble of heart."

Competitiveness and ambition can be healthy traits but not when they become so intense that they lead us to disregard not only the law but also our own safety and the safety of those around us. Jesus calls on us to learn from him gentleness and humility; where better to practice those traits than behind the wheel?

ACT

I will remember that other people are in just as much of a hurry as I am today and defer to others whenever possible. I will pray for patience!

PRAY

Lord Jesus, may I never value my own time and priorities over the well-being of others. Rather, teach me to imitate you in gentleness and humility, not obstructing and endangering others but helping them on their way. Amen.

Thursday, December 14
Second Week of Advent

BEGIN

Be silent. Be still. Pray, "Come, Lord Jesus!"

PRAY

I am the LORD, your God,
who grasps your right hand;
it is I who say to you, "Fear not,
I will help you."

~*Isaiah 41:13*

LISTEN

Read Matthew 11:11–15.

"If you are willing to accept it, he is Elijah, the one
who is to come."

~*Matthew 11:14*

"Whoever Has Ears Ought to Hear"

I stumbled on the website of a wedding photographer
that included advice on how a couple can plan a great
exit from their reception: the timing, the pace, the spar-
klers, and the bubbles—that sort of thing. But no amount
of planning can match the exit of the prophet Elijah in
the ninth century BC. According to the Second Book of
Kings, Elijah didn't simply die; he was taken living into
heaven in a chariot of fire.

A part of Jewish tradition concerning Elijah is that he
will return to earth to herald the coming of the Messiah.
This tradition is the background for the startling remark
Jesus makes, regarding John the Baptist, in today's gospel reading: "He is Elijah, . . . the one who is to come."

There are varying interpretations of what Jesus was saying about John; did Jesus mean literally that John *was* Elijah, or did he mean that the ministry of Elijah had been revitalized in John? John certainly was *like* Elijah, an uncompromising prophet who spoke the truth, even if it irritated the king. Anticipating the coming of the Messiah, John preached reform and personal integrity, regardless of how people received him. Even in prison he did not waver from what he understood to be his mission.

In his unwavering and unhidden devotion to God and principle, John was a role model for us who live in a culture that is often indifferent or even hostile to Christian faith and morality. People who came in contact with John had no trouble discerning what he believed. May that be said of us as well!

ACT

I will watch for one opportunity today to give witness to the coming of Christ. This may be as simple as being charitable toward a store clerk or as explicit as talking about my faith at work. If I fail today, I will plan something more explicit for tomorrow.

PRAY

Lord Jesus, John the Baptist prepared your way by condemning hypocrisy and arrogance and by calling people to reform their lives. May I share in his zeal and imitate his constancy as I help build up your kingdom on earth. Amen.

Friday, December 15

Second Week of Advent

BEGIN

Be silent. Be still. Pray, "Come, Lord Jesus!"

PRAY

I, the LORD, your God,
teach you what is for your good,
and lead you on the way you should go.

~Isaiah 48:17

LISTEN

Read Matthew 11:16–19.

"Wisdom is vindicated by her works."

~Matthew 11:19

The Lord of the Dance

Students of homiletics are often told that their preaching should include everyday images that a congregation will recognize. It's a principle that Jesus often applied, as he does in today's gospel passage, when he observes children playing in the marketplace.

The children, who are taunting unresponsive friends, have been pretending to be adults—alternately playing pipes as though at a celebration and singing dirges as though at a funeral. But their peers won't join in, neither dancing to the joyous music nor wailing—as was the custom at the time—to the mournful song.

Jesus uses the image of these children as a metaphor for "this breed," as he calls them, namely, the people who brushed off the fiery message of repentance preached by John the Baptist and shrugged at the Good News of salvation proclaimed by Jesus himself.

That sort of indifference was not unique to "the breed" of Jesus' time; we see it all around us today. But as disciples who await both the celebration of Jesus' birth and his coming at the end of time, we are called to be anything but indifferent.

We are called to total commitment to the self-evaluation and reform that John preached and the unconditional love of God and neighbor that Jesus called the greatest commandments. What better time is there than Advent to hear the music and join the dance?

ACT

Today, I will be content with rejoicing in the beauty of this season and the rich blessings of my life. I will work at sharing joy with all whom I encounter and give myself completely to Christ as his faithful disciple.

PRAY

O God, send your Holy Spirit to fill my heart so that I may not be a lukewarm Christian but a fully committed disciple of your Son, whose birth we soon will celebrate. May I clearly hear and unflinchingly live his Gospel of love, mercy, and justice. Amen.

Saturday, December 16
Second Week of Advent

BEGIN

Be silent. Be still. Pray, "Come, Lord Jesus!"

PRAY

O shepherd of Israel, hearken,
from your throne upon the cherubim, shine forth.
Rouse your power, and come to save us.

~Psalm 80:2–3

LISTEN

Read Matthew 17:10–13.

"I tell you that Elijah has already come, and they
did not recognize him but did to him whatever they
pleased."

~Matthew 17:12

No Bed of Roses

Joe South wrote a hit song in 1969, "I Never Promised
You a Rose Garden," and that could be the theme of
today's gospel passage. This conversation occurs imme-
diately after the Transfiguration—when James, John, and
Peter saw Jesus speaking with Moses and Elijah, and
Peter wanted to keep the moment going indefinitely.

With Elijah still on their minds after this astounding event, the apostles ask Jesus about the tradition that
Elijah would return before "the great and terrible day of
the LORD," as the prophet Malachi put it (4:5).

Jesus, as we noted yesterday, identified the return of
Elijah with the ministry of John the Baptist who, by the
time of the Transfiguration, had been executed by Herod

Antipas. And that's not the worst of it. Jesus tells the trio: "So also will the Son of Man suffer at their hands" (Matthew 17:12).

The gospels tell us that this kind of talk scandalized the apostles, who seemed to think that Jesus, and they, were bound for glory on a smooth path. But Jesus reminded them on several occasions that anyone who sincerely took on discipleship should expect indifference, ridicule, resistance, and even violent opposition. His disciples were not to be discouraged, nor were they to forsake their faith in order to avoid its challenging consequences.

Rather, the disciples of Jesus were to lead lives of integrity and service, no matter how that might conflict with their own convenience or the current mores of society. As we approach Christmas and the charming baby on his bed of hay, that's what he will call us to once again—integrity and service.

How will we answer?

ACT

I will serve others today, motivated by the unconditional love Jesus preached, and I will not be discouraged by ingratitude, criticism, or cynicism.

PRAY

Lord Jesus, you set a sublime example of service to others despite the opposition of those who did not understand. May I have the fortitude to persist in living with integrity, helping those in need in any way I can, and doing all in your blessed name. Amen.

Sunday, December 17
Third Week of Advent

BEGIN

Be silent. Be still. Pray, "Come, Lord Jesus!"

PRAY

The mighty one has done great things for me,
and holy is his name.

~Luke 1:49

LISTEN

Read John 1:6–8, 19–28.

"I am the voice of one crying out in the desert, 'make
straight the way of the Lord.'"

~John 1:23

Joy, Joy, Joy!

There's nothing subtle about the Church's message on
this Sunday.

In the entrance antiphon, we hear, "Rejoice in the
Lord, always." In the prophecy of Isaiah, we read, "I
rejoice heartily in the Lord." In the psalm response
derived from Luke's gospel, we read, "My spirit rejoices
in God my savior." And in Paul's letter to the church in
Thessalonica we read, "Rejoice always."

This is traditionally called "Gaudete Sunday";
"gaudete" means "rejoice" because our celebration of
the birth of Jesus is drawing near. We can consider the
world around us—and perhaps our personal lives—and
find reasons to opt out of rejoicing. But the joy of this
season doesn't have to do with the highs and lows of
life today; it has to do with the Good News that God is

born into the world to overcome for us the consequences of sin and death—to make possible for us eternal life in his presence.

Father Alfred Delp, a Jesuit who was condemned to death in Germany for participating in resistance to the Nazis, wrote about Advent while he was in prison: "May the time never come when men forget about the good tidings and promises, when so immured within the four walls of their prison, they see nothing but gray days through barred windows placed too high to see out of."

Even to a man about to die, the "good tidings and promises" that would be fulfilled in the ministry, sacrifice, and glorification of Jesus were the focus of this season and the only reason for his joy. May we follow his holy example.

ACT

When I am engaged in any activity in preparation for Christmas during this last week of Advent, I will pause each day to joyously remember what God has done for me.

PRAY

Almighty God, as I experience the benefits and limitations of everyday life, I give you thanks for the promise of a life free from care, and I rejoice as I celebrate the fulfillment of that promise, made visible in the birth of your Son, Jesus Christ. Amen.

Monday, December 18
Third Week of Advent

BEGIN

Be silent. Be still. Pray, "Come, Lord Jesus!"

PRAY

As king he shall reign and govern wisely,
he shall do what is just and right in the land.

~Jeremiah 23:5

LISTEN

Read Matthew 1:18–24.

"Joseph, son of David, do not be afraid to take Mary
your wife into your home. For it is through the Holy
Spirit that this child has conceived in her. . . . You are
to name him Jesus, because he will save his people
from their sins."

~Matthew 1:20–21

To Do God's Will

One of my regrets is that I don't know anything about
the circumstances of my birth except what's on my birth
certificate. I don't know whether I have forgotten the
details my mother told me or whether she didn't tell me
anything. Perhaps I never asked her.

There's a historical context to every child's birth, of
course; I was born nine months into World War II, for
example, and I imagine that was an anxious time for new
parents who didn't know how war would affect them
and their children.

Was I early; was I late? Who took care of my older
brother while Mom was in the hospital? Who was there

to greet me when she brought me home? Who picked the name? I'll never know.

Fortunately, we are not in the dark about the birth of Jesus. We know what we need to know. And one of the things we know is that Joseph, whose life was turned upside down by the manner in which Jesus was conceived, did not concern himself with the disruption of his plans but with what his conscience told him was right. His first instinct was to protect Mary from public scandal or worse, so when he discerned the will of God he did not hesitate but acted.

How often do we know in our hearts what God would want from us in a given situation but do not act because acting would change our plans, eat into our resources, or make us confront something difficult or unpleasant?

Joseph disappears from the biblical narrative long before Jesus begins his public ministry, but Joseph is a model for all who know God's will for them and find the courage to act on it, no matter the likely costs.

ACT

When I hear God's call to discipleship in my parish, community, or workplace and know I have the wherewithal to respond, I will not put my own comfort and convenience before his will.

PRAY

Almighty God, St. Joseph accepted the critical role of spouse of the Virgin Mary and guardian of the child Jesus because he understood this to be your will. Whenever I sense in my heart that you are calling me to service, may I respond as Joseph did, taking on whatever you ask of me for the good of others. Amen.

TUESDAY, DECEMBER 19
THIRD WEEK OF ADVENT

BEGIN

Be silent. Be still. Pray, "Come, Lord Jesus!"

PRAY

O God, you have taught me from my youth,
and till the present I proclaim your wondrous deeds.

~Psalm 71:17

LISTEN

Read Luke 1:5–25.

In the days of Herod, King of Judea, there was a
priest named Zechariah. . . . His wife was . . . Elizabeth. Both were righteous in the eyes of God,
observing all the commandments and ordinances of
the Lord.

~Luke 1:5–6

God Remembers

More than thirty men in the scriptures had the name
Zechariah or a derivative of it. The name comes from a
Hebrew word that means "God has remembered." How
apropos that is to the situation of Zechariah and his wife
Elizabeth, the parents of John the Baptist! As today's
gospel passage records, they had no children and were
beyond childbearing years. In their culture, that was a
calamity in a couple's lives, commonly interpreted as a
burden imposed by God. And yet we read that Zechariah faithfully served God in the Temple and that Elizabeth and he were people who lived by God's Law.

Most of us experience disappointment in life and, even if we don't feel disappointed, most of us can name some ways in which our lives could have been better. To put it another way, no one leads a perfect life in this world. Yet we are promised a perfect life, but that is eternal life in the presence of God, made possible by the ministry and sacrifice of Jesus, whose birth we will celebrate next Monday.

Luke's account implies that, despite their disappointment, Zechariah and Elizabeth remained faithful to God. God remembered and blessed them with a son, and not just any son. And we can be sure that God remembered and welcomed them into heaven.

This last week of Advent, may we thank God for what we have in this life but, more important, recommit ourselves to live, as Jesus taught us, lives of generosity and mercy, confident that when we leave this imperfect life, God will remember.

ACT

Today I will silently express my gratitude to God for the positive things, large and small, that bless my life, especially for the gift of his Son, Jesus Christ.

PRAY

Almighty God, you set humans as stewards over creation, not so that we can fashion a heaven on earth but rather so that we can live in service to you and to each other. Teach me to do my part in caring for creation and to look forward in undying hope to life with you in eternal peace. Amen.

Wednesday, December 20
Third Week of Advent

BEGIN

Be silent. Be still. Pray, "Come, Lord Jesus!"

PRAY

The Lord's are the earth and its fullness;
the world and those who dwell in it.

~Psalm 24:1

LISTEN

Read Luke 1:26–38.

"The Holy Spirit will come upon you, and the power
of the Most High will overshadow you. . . . Nothing
will be impossible for God."

~Luke 1:35, 37

Possible with God

Physicist Michio Kaku, in his book *The Physics of the
Impossible* speculated as to whether several phenomena
portrayed in science fiction would ever become realities.
For example, he concluded that teleportation is possible
and that foreseeing the future is not. Kaku based his
findings on what human beings might do within the
known laws of physics.

The archangel Gabriel, on the other hand, in his
statement in today's gospel passage, talked about what
God can do, often through the cooperation of human
beings: God can be born into human history through the
cooperation of the Virgin Mary.

Today, the World Food Programme (WFP) estimates
that about 795 million people worldwide do not have

enough food to lead a healthy life. The problem is so large that it's impossible to solve.

Or is it? The WFP and Pope Francis, among others, point out that there are enough resources to feed everyone in the world. For example, the USDA estimates that we in the United States throw out 30 to 40 percent of the food we produce each year. Clearly, what is lacking on the part of those who do have enough to eat is the will to find creative solutions for feeding those who do not. Pope Francis has said that we first must stop accepting hunger as normal and inevitable.

We know from what Jesus did and taught that God wants us to feed the poor. To do so, we have to imitate the generosity of God made manifest by his creation of which we are part and in sending his only Son, Jesus Christ, to redeem us from the consequences of sin.

It's up to each of us to recognize in our hearts what part we can play in sharing God's generosity with people in need.

ACT

Today I will take one specific action to help address hunger in my community. I can research the problem or contact a service agency and offer to help. I will not accept hunger and other forms of want as economically or politically unavoidable.

PRAY

Creator God, help me remain thankful for the abundance of this world, and in gratitude for your generosity, teach me to share what I have with those who are in need. Make me an instrument of your justice and compassion. Amen.

Thursday, December 21
Third Week of Advent

BEGIN

Be silent. Be still. Pray, "Come, Lord Jesus!"

PRAY

The plan of the Lord stands forever;
the design of his heart, through all generations.

~Psalm 33:11

LISTEN

Read Luke 1:39–45.

"Blessed are you who believed that what was spoken
to you by the Lord, would be fulfilled."

~ Luke 1:45

Seize the Day

"It will be over before you know it" is a running joke in
our family, brought out whenever we discuss preparations for a holiday or another complicated event. The
implication, of course, is that we're going through a lot
of trouble, and often building up a lot of angst, over
something that will last only a few hours.

We shouldn't let that apply to our observance of the
Nativity. Rather, our observance should be in the spirit in
which Elizabeth greeted Mary: "The moment the sound
of your greeting reached my ears, the infant in my womb
leaped for joy."

The exuberance of Mary in immediately traveling
nearly a hundred miles to visit Elizabeth, the enthusiasm
with which Elizabeth greeted her kinswoman, and the
instinctive leap of the unborn John the Baptist are the

kinds of emotions that should accompany our celebration of Christ's coming.

Perhaps we grow tired of being reminded year after year of the "reason for the season," but the duration and intensity of the merchandising of Christmas makes those reminders more necessary than ever. Each of us, by the joy and reverence with which we anticipate the rapidly approaching holy day, can help to spread the true devotion due this observance.

By attending to the profound meanings of this season, we can help others also embrace the birth of our Savior—yesterday, today, and at the end of time—and contemplate his message of hope, justice, and peace rather than wishing that the whole Christmas rush were over.

ACT

During these last few days of Advent, I will create around me an atmosphere of peace and anticipation so that others may more readily experience the true spirit of Christmas.

PRAY

Almighty God, my gratitude for the gift of your Son, our Savior, will be reflected in the spirit with which I celebrate his birth. May he be the center of my life, now and always. Amen.

Friday, December 22
Third Week of Advent

BEGIN

Be silent. Be still. Pray, "Come, Lord Jesus!"

PRAY

The LORD puts to death and gives life;
he casts down to the nether world;
he raises up again.

~1 Samuel 2:6

LISTEN

Read Luke 1:46–56.

"The Almighty has done great things for me, and
holy is his name."

~Luke 1:49

Only One Mary

Ludwig van Beethoven once wrote to a wealthy patron who irritated him, "Prince, what you are, you are through chance and birth; what I am, I am through my own labor. There are many princes and there will be thousands more, but there is only one Beethoven."

However justified Beethoven may have been, his attitude stands in marked contrast to the tone of Mary's *Magnificat*. In Mary's hymn, as presented by Luke, she anticipates the unique place she will occupy in the minds of generations to come, but she magnifies the Lord, not herself. It is God who has looked with favor on her, God who has done great things for her, and God, as the hymn goes on to say, who is the author of all that is good in the world.

We praise and revere Mary for her status as the mother of our Savior; we follow her as the first of her son's disciples and laud her witness to his death and resurrection. We turn to Mary in prayer to intercede for us with the Lord.

But we also honor her and hope to emulate her for her humble submission to God's will and her gratitude for his blessings.

The popes, especially since the mid-twentieth century, have had a particular devotion to Mary, perhaps recognizing a kinship with a human being who has willingly taken on such a profound mission from God and humbly accepted the mantle of leadership. Each of us can share in this kinship if we listen carefully to God's voice and say yes to his call—not as we will but as he wills.

ACT

Today I will take note of my talents and abilities and strive to remain confident in them. I will thank God for his kindness toward me and be mindful of my dependence on God for all things.

PRAY

Mary, our mother, during this season I am keenly aware of your place in the history of our salvation. May I always honor you, imitate you, and turn to you in prayer as I seek the mercy of Jesus, your son and our Lord. Amen.

Saturday, December 23
Third Week of Advent

BEGIN

Be silent. Be still. Pray, "Come, Lord Jesus!"

PRAY

All the paths of the Lord are kindness and constancy
toward those who keep his covenant and his decrees.

~Psalm 25:10

LISTEN

Read Luke 1:57–66.

All who heard these things took them to heart,
saying, "What, then, will this child be? For surely the
hand of the Lord was with him."

~Luke 1:66

God Is Gracious

My nephew's name was Anthony; his father, my brother,
was Anthony Louis. Our father was Anthony Louis; and
his father, Dominick. Dominick's father was Luigi Anto-
nio; and his father, Dominick. Get the picture? That's the
kind of naming tradition that arises in the story we read
in today's gospel passage.

Luke's account makes clear how deeply imbedded
a similar tradition was in first-century Palestine, when
he reports that the neighbors and relatives of Elizabeth
and Zechariah were "astonished" that the parents would
name their son John rather than honoring Zechariah or
another family member.

The name John—meaning "God is gracious"—was
prescribed by the archangel Gabriel, as we read earlier

in this gospel. The significance of that name for a couple who had believed they would die childless is obvious.

But the birth of John the Baptist transcended the hopes of his parents, because John was to be the bridge between the Covenant with Israel and the Gospel of Jesus Christ. Perhaps the breach in the tradition of family names symbolized John's role, grounded in the Law of Moses but preparing people for a new understanding of God's relationship with not only Israel but also the whole world. John wouldn't preach about tradition; he would preach with urgency, calling his audience to repent and reform their lives in that moment, in expectation of "one who is coming."

As we anticipate our celebration of the coming of that One, let us reflect with urgency on the ways in which our lives might be renewed in light of his Gospel.

ACT

I will devote quiet time during the remaining hours of Advent to contemplating the things I would like to refresh or renew in my relationship with God and with my family, friends, and neighbors.

PRAY

Almighty God, I strive to emulate our ancestors in faith in their devotion to you and to your law. May the coming celebration of Christmas fortify my faith and renew my commitment to build up your kingdom on earth. Amen.

Sunday, December 24
Fourth Week of Advent

BEGIN

Be silent. Be still. Pray, "Come, Lord Jesus!"

PRAY

The promises of the LORD I will sing forever;
through all generations my mouth shall proclaim
your faithfulness.

~Psalm 89:2

LISTEN

Read Luke 1:26–38.

Then the angel said to her, "Do not be afraid, Mary,
for you have found favor with God. Behold, you will
conceive in your womb and bear a son, and you shall
name him Jesus."

~Luke 1:30–31

"Rejoice, O Highly Favored"

There is a jarring contrast between ideas that appear in
today's gospel passage.

First, the archangel Gabriel begins his visit to Mary
with a series of upbeat remarks: She is to rejoice, she is
"highly favored," the Lord is with her, and she is blessed
among women. But the evangelist's next statement
doesn't seem to follow logically on all that good news:
"She was greatly troubled at what was said."

It would be understandable if Mary were amazed,
even frightened. But why was she troubled? Perhaps
Gabriel's compliments didn't dispel a premonition
that she was about to be called by God to take on an

inexplicable, awkward, and even dangerous responsibility. And when Gabriel has spelled out exactly such a responsibility, Mary's acquiescence ("May it be done to me . . .") seems rather abrupt.

Maybe we shouldn't take too literally the time frame in which these events seem to have occurred; perhaps Mary came more gradually to understand God's will, and maybe she deliberated a little longer before she said yes. After all, Luke was describing a unique situation that had unique dynamics. But we, like Mary, are human beings; we, like Mary, have free wills; and we, like Mary, are called to serve God—often in ways that we might not have chosen for ourselves.

An angel needn't call. We know what God wants of us—to serve him and to serve each other. Every day brings fresh opportunities to say yes.

ACT

In the midst of final Christmas preparations and likely celebrations, I will be mindful today of God's voice calling me to him and my neighbor, and even if I falter I will always renew my yes.

PRAY

Almighty God, thank you for the gift of the Virgin Mary who willingly gave birth to your Son, cared for him as he grew and learned, and became his disciple when he taught his message of justice and love. May I be worthy of my spiritual mother, saying yes, as she did, when you call. Amen.

Monday, December 25
The Nativity of the Lord

BEGIN

Be silent. Be still. Pray, "Come, Lord Jesus!"

PRAY

Announce his salvation, day after day.
Tell his glory among the nations;
Among all peoples, his wondrous deeds.

~Psalm 96:2–3

LISTEN

Read Luke 2:1–14 (Mass at Midnight).

The angel said to them, "Do not be afraid; for behold,
I proclaim to you good news of great joy that will be
for all the people."

~Luke 2:10

A Savior Has Been Born

A researcher at Washington and Lee University reported
in 2014 that less than 9 percent of television Christmas
specials broadcast in the 1960s referred in a substantial
way to the religious basis for the holiday. One of the few
was *A Charlie Brown Christmas*, first aired in 1965 by a
reluctant CBS network amid predictions that it would be
a failure. The reticence of the network and the producers
was due in part to a scene in which the *Peanuts* character
Linus recites seven verses from the Gospel according to
Luke—the account, included in today's reading, of the
annunciation to the shepherds. The program has been
broadcast every year since and is for many people an
indispensable part of the season.

How contradictory that the television professionals thought a special prompted in the first place by the birth of Jesus would be doomed if Jesus played any part in it. But Christmas is here, and Jesus is its reason for being and its message. We know now that it doesn't matter if the pageant was a little shaky, the lights were a little garish, or the tree was a little scrawny. What matters is that the Son of God was born into the world, that he taught us to bring peace and love to each other, that he gave his own life so we might live forever in heaven, and that he lives among us still in his body and blood, in his word, and in his Church.

"That's what Christmas is all about, Charlie Brown!"

ACT

No matter what goes wrong today and for the rest of the year, I will rejoice with the angels that Jesus Christ is born!

PRAY

Lord, Jesus Christ, I celebrate your birth today, and I hope to share my joy with others, today and every day. Be born into the world again and again through my acts of kindness, generosity, and justice, you who live and reign with the Father and the Holy Spirit now and forever. Amen.

THE PSALMS OF CHRISTMAS

Next to the yearly celebration of the paschal mystery, the Church holds most sacred the memorial of Christ's birth and early manifestations. This is the purpose of the Christmas season. The Christmas season runs from Evening Prayer I of Christmas until the Sunday after Epiphany or after January 6, inclusive. The Mass of the Vigil of Christmas is used in the evening of December 24, either before or after Evening Prayer I. On Christmas itself, following an ancient tradition of Rome, three Masses may be celebrated: namely, the Mass at Midnight, the Mass at Dawn, and the Mass during the Day.

—*General Norms for the Liturgical Year and the Calendar, 32-34*

On the following pages we offer you the Responsorial Psalms for the four Masses of Christmas. May they fill your Christmas season with boundless joy and deepest peace.

Christmas, Vigil Mass

Responsorial Psalm   Ps 89:4–5, 16–17, 27, 29

R. For ever I will sing the goodness of the Lord.
I have made a covenant with my chosen one,
    I have sworn to David my servant:
forever will I confirm your posterity
    and establish your throne for all generations.

R. For ever I will sing the goodness of the Lord.
Blessed the people who know the joyful shout;
    in the light of your countenance, O Lord, they walk.
At your name they rejoice all the day,
    and through your justice they are exalted.

R. For ever I will sing the goodness of the Lord.
He shall say of me, "You are my father,
    my God, the rock, my savior."
Forever I will maintain my kindness toward him,
    and my covenant with him stands firm.

R. For ever I will sing the goodness of the Lord.

Mass at Midnight

Responsorial Psalm   Ps 96: 1–2, 2–3, 11–12, 13

R. Today is born our Savior, Christ the Lord.
Sing to the Lord a new song;
    sing to the Lord, all you lands.
Sing to the Lord; bless his name.

R. Today is born our Savior, Christ the Lord.
Announce his salvation, day after day.
    Tell his glory among the nations;
    among all peoples, his wondrous deeds.

R. Today is born our Savior, Christ the Lord.
Let the heavens be glad and the earth rejoice;
    let the sea and what fills it resound;
    let the plains be joyful and all that is in them!
Then shall all the trees of the forest exult.

R. Today is born our Savior, Christ the Lord.
They shall exult before the Lord, for he comes;
    for he comes to rule the earth.
He shall rule the world with justice
    and the peoples with his constancy.

R. Today is born our Savior, Christ the Lord.

Mass at Dawn

Responsorial Psalm   Ps 97:1, 6, 11–12

R. A light will shine on us this day: the Lord is born for us.
The LORD is king; let the earth rejoice;
    let the many isles be glad.
The heavens proclaim his justice,
    and all peoples see his glory.

R. A light will shine on us this day: the Lord is born for us.
Light dawns for the just;
    and gladness, for the upright of heart.
Be glad in the LORD, you just,
    and give thanks to his holy name.

R. A light will shine on us this day: the Lord is born for us.

Mass during the Day

Responsorial Psalm   **Ps 98:1, 2–3, 3–4, 5–6**

R. All the ends of the earth have seen the saving power of God.
Sing to the Lord a new song,
    for he has done wondrous deeds;
his right hand has won victory for him,
    his holy arm.

R. All the ends of the earth have seen the saving power of God.
The Lord has made his salvation known:
    in the sight of the nations he has revealed his
    justice.
He has remembered his kindness and his faithfulness
    toward the house of Israel.

R. All the ends of the earth have seen the saving power of God.
All the ends of the earth have seen
    the salvation by our God.
Sing joyfully to the Lord, all you lands;
    break into song; sing praise.

R. All the ends of the earth have seen the saving power of God.
Sing praise to the Lord with the harp,
    with the harp and melodious song.
With trumpets and the sound of the horn
    sing joyfully before the King, the Lord.

R. All the ends of the earth have seen the saving power of God.

Charles Paolino is managing editor at RENEW International. He is a permanent deacon of the Diocese of Metuchen, New Jersey, ministering in liturgy, preaching, and adult education at Our Lady of Lourdes Church in Whitehouse Station. He also is a columnist for *The Catholic Spirit*—the newspaper and website of the Diocese of Metuchen—and a freelance theater critic.

Paolino spent forty-three years in newspaper journalism and more than thirty years as an adjunct instructor of English at various universities and colleges, including Seton Hall and Rutgers. He earned a bachelor's degree in communications from Seton Hall and a master's degree in journalism from Penn State. He and his wife, Patricia Ann, live in Whitehouse Station. They have four grown children and five grandchildren.

AVE

AVE MARIA PRESS

Founded in 1865, Ave Maria Press,
a ministry of the Congregation of
Holy Cross, is a Catholic publishing
company that serves the spiritual and
formative needs of the Church and its
schools, institutions, and ministers;
Christian individuals and families; and
others seeking spiritual nourishment.

For a complete listing of titles from

Ave Maria Press

Sorin Books

Forest of Peace

Christian Classics

visit www.avemariapress.com

AVE MARIA PRESS
Notre Dame, IN
A Ministry of the United States Province of Holy Cross